Mary, Queen Of Scots & Elizabeth I, Queen And The Stuart And Tudor Dynasties

Introduction

From the day she was born in 1542, Mary, Queen of Scots had a claim to the English throne as Henry VIII's sister Margaret had married Mary's grandfather, James IV of Scotland.

As a consequence of this claim, whenever Henry's daughter Elizabeth became Queen of England in 1558 potential for conflict between Mary and Elizabeth, existed.

Before Mary ever crossed the border into England to seek refuge with Elizabeth both of them had already had to cope with disappointment and trouble from very early on in life.

Mary was only a few days old when her father, James V, died. At the age of six, for her own safety, she was packed off to France, only returning to Scotland in 1561.

Elizabeth was three years old when her mother, Anne Boleyn, was executed. Rather than caring for the young Elizabeth her father Henry's main goal in life was finding a replacement for her mother, someone who would provide him with the male heir he desired.

On returning from France, Mary spent only a further seven short, but eventful years back at home. It is probably not commonly realised just how little of her adult life Mary spent in Scotland. As the pictures will show the days visiting friends must have been amongst the happiest of Mary's life.

When she lands in England in 1568, Mary places herself at the "mercy" of not only Elizabeth but Elizabeth's advisors. Mercy in those days was expected only from God. In royal circles in particular, little reason or no reason was required to justify the disposal of an opponent or anyone else for that matter, the favoured method being execution.

The days Elizabeth had spent in the Tower of London during her half sister Mary I's reign and the three marriages which Mary, Queen of Scots had had must have brought home to both of them how things can go horribly wrong without a great deal of personal input.

As her period in captivity lengthens, one can understand why, despite the obvious risks, Mary becomes increasingly more desperate, clutching at any prospect, any remote means, by which she might regain her freedom. She is easy prey.

Equally so, we can see how, as each plot unfolds or is engineered by her advisors, Elizabeth is eventually forced to act, against her better judgement, later blaming everyone but herself for the implementation of the warrant she has signed.

The front entrance to Craigmillar Castle, the favourite residence of Mary as a child. Her ministers planned Lord Darnley's death there and Mary lived there with The Earl of Bothwell.

THE AUTHOR

MY INTEREST IN HISTORY

As far back as I can remember I have been interested in history. As a child this was due to visits to Stirling Castle, Edinburgh Castle, the Tower of London and Westminster Abbey.

Stories about Mary, Queen of Scots, Bonnie Prince Charlie, and Henry VIII and his six wives were more interesting than fiction.

Born and brought up on the banks of the River Leven which flows out of Loch Lomond, world famous for it's beauty and now also known for it's golf course, my interest in history was not surprising. That famous outlaw and folk hero Rob Roy was born a few miles away. Mary, Queen of Scots, had escaped from Dumbarton Castle in 1548 and made her way to France. It was at Stirling Bridge that William Wallace had his famous victory over King Edward I of England in 1297. Dumbarton Castle had had other famous visitors down through the centuries – the Vikings in 870, Kings of Scotland, prisoners such as the Jacobites after the '45 and the French during the Napoleonic Wars.

In 1310 Robert Bruce was crowned King Robert I of Scotland following which in 1314 he defeated King Edward II at the Battle of Bannockburn. A famous Scottish victory arguably more important than Wembley in 1967. In 1329 Robert died at Cardross Castle about six miles from Loch Lomond.

Anyone, who like me, is fortunate enough to live and work in Argyll, is surrounded by remarkable scenery and places of historical significance. How can one fail to appreciate the hills and glens, looking across the Firth of Clyde to the Cloch Lighthouse, going past Loch Eck to Inveraray, or taking the Waverley trip round the Kyles of Bute? On Dunoon's Castlehill, Robert Burns's "Bonnie Mary of Argyll" looks down river in his direction, towards Ayrshire.

Inveraray Castle has been a home of Clan Campbell and successive Earls and Dukes of Argyll since the end of the 15th century. Many generations of the Campbell family have made important contributions to Scottish history and to British history.

Rothesay Castle, on the island of Bute, and Paisley Abbey have long been associated with the Stewarts, hereditary Stewards of the Kings of Scotland and from 1371 the royal house of Scotland.

It was the son of the marriage of Robert the Bruce's daughter Marjorie to Walter the 6th Steward who established the House of Stewart or Stuart to which all Scottish monarchs could trace their ancestry. Their son became King Robert II of Scotland.

By around 1200 the island of Bute was held by Alan, the "Steward" of King William I of Scotland, William the Lion. Alan's father, Walter the 1st High Steward of Scotland, founded Paisley Abbey by charter in 1163. Buried in the Abbey are six High Stewards of the Kings of Scotland, Marjorie Bruce and King Robert III.

Descended from Sir John Stewart, a son of King Robert II, is the present Marquess of Bute, John Colum Crichton Stuart, the 7th Marquess of Bute of Mount Stuart, Bute.

Inveraray Castle, Rothesay Castle, Mount Stuart and Paisley Abbey are all open to the public and popular tourist destinations.

Charles, Prince of Wales, is the present Duke of Rothesay.

***Stirling Castle**, where Mary, Queen of Scots was crowned on 9 September 1543. The baptism of her son, James VI and I was celebrated there in December, 1566.*

HISTORICAL DOCUMENTS AND THIS BOOKLET

My first serious venture into historical documents was the purchase of letters at Bloomsbury Auctions in London in 2002.

These were hand written letters – signed or unsigned depending upon whether or not he wished to remain anonymous – sent by Prince Charles Edward Stuart in 1746/48 while he was on the run after Culloden. The recipients were King Louis XV of France and his secretary.

Copies of the same letters, sent at the same time by Charles to his father, were bought later, in Rome, by King George IV and are now in the Royal Archives in Windsor Castle.

I bought six letters, the others going to a dealer in the room and an anonymous bidder on the telephone.

My letters are the originals! The Queen has the copies sent to the Old Pretender!

Subsequent visits to Christie's for "The Spiro Collection" in 2003, and in 2008, and to Bonhams for "The Enys Collection" in 2004, have provided the backbone to my Scottish documents. The acknowledgements on the inside front cover give an indication of some of the other sources from which documents have been acquired.

Hardly does a day pass but my daughter shows me a newspaper article or my wife draws my attention to a report on the teletext about some letter or document that is for sale; and I often have something similar.

Visits to Edinburgh Castle, Culloden, and other historical sites have brought home to me the fact that few historical documents are on view anywhere.

It is the continuing public interest in historical documents and the lack of material on display that have convinced me that this booklet, based upon my documents, might engender sufficient interest as to make it worthwhile.

History has always seemed to me to be a rich source of information as far as most subjects are concerned, culture, religion, politics, etc. Now that history seems to have been relegated as far as the school curriculum is concerned, perhaps this booklet might also be of interest to pupils.

What is certain is that, from now on, new hand written material, including historical documents, will cease to exist. It is a matter of opinion, of course, as to whether this is important. However there is nothing quite like handling paperwork which has been written or signed by Queen Elizabeth I of England, Mary. Queen of Scots, Sir Winston Churchill or Robert Burns. Not only hand written but printed books and even bookstores are now under threat of extinction such is the speed of "progress".

Since Mary, Queen of Scots, is the principal character in this booklet, Queen Elizabeth I has to be the chief supporting character because their lives were so intertwined, and James VI did succeed Elizabeth I as James I when the crowns were united.

Tudor material available will facilitate the production of a complementary booklet in which the roles will be reversed with Elizabeth I, the main character.

Edinburgh Castle, where Mary, Queen of Scots, gave birth to James VI on 19 June 1566. The Honours of Scotland – the Crown, Sceptre and Sword of State, the United Kingdom's oldest royal regalia - are housed there.

Dumbarton Castle, *from where Mary, Queen of Scots, aged 6 years, escaped to France in 1548. The town of Dumbarton, which is situated at the point where the river Leven, flowing from Loch Lomond joins the river Clyde, was the ancient Capital of Strathclyde.*

Mary, Queen of Scots & Elizabeth I, Queen of England

The story of Mary, Queen of Scots, and her involvement with Elizabeth I, Queen of England is a tragic one.

In order to recount Mary's story there are incorporated here original documents relating to Mary, her three husbands, her family and associates and other Scottish documents from the sixteenth century.

Also included are documents signed by Queen Elizabeth I, her father King Henry VIII, her half brother and half sister, King Edward VI and Queen Mary I respectively, and other important individuals from Tudor times.

Mary was born in Linlithgow Palace in 1542 to James V of Scotland and his second wife, Mary of Guise.

She was not only heir to the throne of Scotland but, as a result of her grandfather James IV's marriage to Margaret Tudor, she also had a claim to the throne of England. Margaret Tudor was the daughter of Henry VII and sister of Henry VIII. The marriage is known as the Union of the Thistle and the Rose.

It was the 100 year period between that marriage in 1503 and "the Union of the Crowns" in 1603 when James VI of Scotland became James I of England that was to see great changes in the affairs of Scotland and England.

The changes not only involved the monarchy but reformation in the church. The Reformation started in various parts of Europe when Martin Luther, amongst others, spearheaded revolt against arrogance and corruption in the church in Rome.

In England Henry VIII declared himself Head of the Church. In Scotland it was John Knox, a Roman Catholic priest, who became a follower of John Calvin and was instrumental in bringing about change.

Henry VII of England

The first document featured is one signed by King Henry VII. It was he who put an end to the Wars of the Roses when he defeated Richard III at the Battle of Bosworth in 1485. This rivalry ceased when Henry VII (of Lancaster) married Elizabeth of York in the following year.

In this context recent archaeological digs at Bosworth in Leicestershire have uncovered bones thought to be those of Richard III who was buried on the battlefield.

This is Henry VII's signature cut from a letter to King John of Denmark, Sweden, and Norway. It is dated 11 November 1506 with papered seal. He signs with a full signature, very often he only used his initials.

In order to curb the power of the Lords, Henry set up a court known as a Star Chamber. During his reign Christopher Columbus discovered America. Henry encouraged exploration and expanded the English fleet.

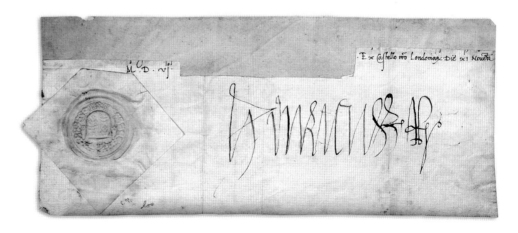

James IV and his Great Seal

James IV was King of Scotland from 1488 to 1513. He was the son of James III who was assassinated after the Battle of Sauchieburn by someone posing as a priest.

The following document on vellum shows the Great Seal of James IV. It is a royal grant of James IV at Edinburgh, 3 March 1504, to John Sinclare of Hurdmanstoun of all the lands of Hurdmanstoun with castle, fortalice and mill, together with the rights of patronage, advowson and donation of the Chapel of St John the Evangelist, near the castle lying within our shire of Edinburgh.

Paisley Abbey *founded by Charter at Fotheringhay Castle in 1163.*

The tombstone of John Hamilton, Abbot of Paisley Abbey and Archbishop of St Andrews.

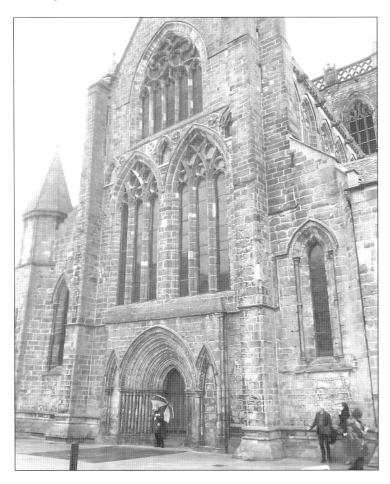

James IV contributed to building costs at Paisley Abbey. His advisor, Abbot George Shaw, the Treasurer of Scotland, was present at the Battle of Sauchieburn. Abbot John Hamilton, a supporter of Mary, Queen of Scots became Archbishop of St. Andrews. He was hanged at Stirling in 1571 for his involvement in the murders of Lord Darnley and the Earl of Moray. The inscription on his tombstone above translates to 'Mercy and peace'.

The early Stewarts had a long association with Rothesay Castle. Robert II, grandson of Robert Bruce spent much of his time here. It was James IV and James V who added the large residential gatehouse shown above.

JAMES IV AND 3RD LORD GRAHAM

I have two documents signed by James IV.

The first letter (from Edinburgh) c.1500 was to William, 3rd Lord Graham in connection with land. Lord Graham later became 1st Earl of Montrose and died at James IV's side at Flodden in 1513. Another nobleman to fall with the King was Archibald Campbell, the 2nd Earl of Argyll. He was the first one of the family to hold the appointment of Master of the Royal Household in Scotland, a position still held today by Torquhil, the 13th Duke of Argyll.

It was during the reign of James IV that the building of the Palace of Holyrood, in Edinburgh, commenced and the production of whisky first came to prominence.

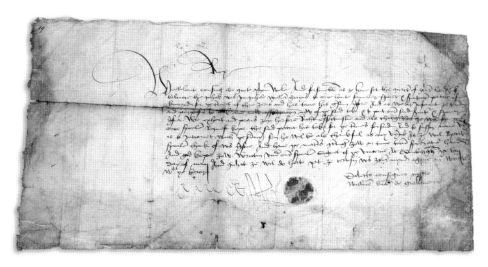

JAMES IV AND LORD LIVINGSTONE

The second letter (from Edinburgh) was written, 3 months before James's death, to William, Lord Livingstone. It orders Livingstone to send his men to join the army being sent to the aid of the King of France. Scotland and France had originally signed the "Auld Alliance" agreement in 1295. This agreement was renewed by James IV and Louis XII of France in July 1512 and it provoked the events which led to Scotland's defeat and James's death at Flodden the next year.

Although it was during the reign of James III that Edinburgh emerged as Scotland's capital and Edinburgh Castle as the most important castle being his residence, it was James IV who completed the remainder of the work required to re-establish the castle as a royal residence. The ancient Honours of Scotland, the oldest regalia in the United Kingdom, reside in the castle.

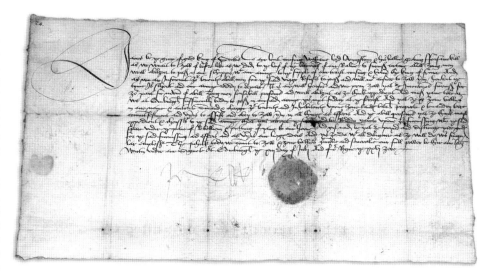

JAMES V AND WILLIAM LIVINGSTONE

Although The Crown was made for James V in 1540 and worn by him at the coronation of Mary of Guise, it was James IV who acquired The SCEPTRE and THE SWORD of STATE. The SCEPTRE was presented to him by Pope Alexander VI around 1494 and THE SWORD by Pope Julius II in 1507. The HONOURS were rediscovered in the castle by Sir Walter Scott prior to the visit of George IV in 1822 and together with the Stone of Destiny can be seen by visitors.

James V, Mary's father, became King of Scotland when he was only 17 months old. As the Tudors were distrusted he was kept well away from his mother as much as possible as he grew up.

James was disliked by the nobility but popular with the peasants. Disguised as a farmer he often moved amongst the peasants, seducing their daughters. James obviously had the same genes as his uncle Henry - Henry VIII. James married Madeleine, daughter of Francis I of France, with whom he forged closer alignment, and following her death, Mary of Guise. In November 1542 the Scottish Army invaded England and was routed at Solway Moss. News of the disaster hastened James's death the following month.

This document written by James's secretary in December 1529 (from Stirling) to William Livingstone of Kilsyth is signed by James and countersigned at the foot. It is a licence for Livingstone and his family and servants to travel on pilgrimage as he pleased. A passport!

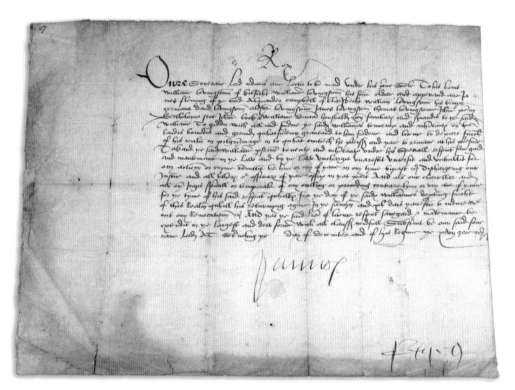

was built by James IV in 1500 to replace the old castle. James V added to it and it was to Falkland Palace James retired after his defeat at Solway Moss. He died there soon after, but not before hearing of the birth of his baby daughter, Mary. The Palace became a favourite of Mary, Queen of Scots, for hawking and hunting. It is open to the public and managed by the National Trust

Falkland village with it's cobbled streets and old houses clustered around the Palace is both historical and delightful. Marriage lintels can be found. The two sets of initials and date may record a marriage, when a house was built or when owners moved in. At the end of the eighteenth century there were 231 weavers in the village, a trade which grew out of the supply of linen to the Palace.

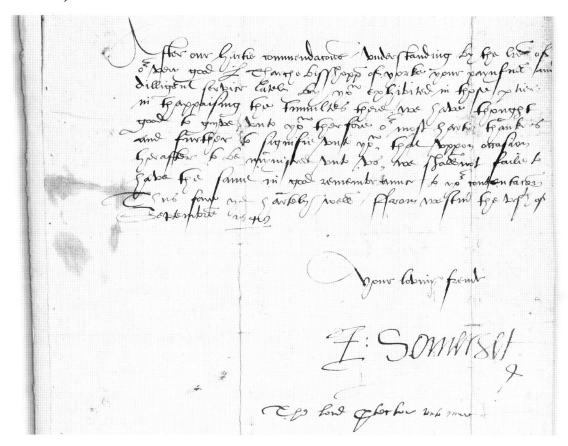

In 1547, after the battle of Pinkie Cleugh, Midlothian, Mary, Queen of Scots, aged 5, was sent for safety to Inchmahome Priory in Perthshire. She was on her way via Dumbarton Castle to France.

The battle was a major triumph for the English troops, under the Duke of Somerset, Regent for the young Edward VI. Somerset was following Henry VIII's policy of roughing up the Scots with a view to forcing the marriage of Mary, Queen of Scots to young Edward.

The above letter, Westminster, 6 September 1549, signed "E Somerset" as Lord Protector is to Richard Bunny, treasurer of Berwick thanking him for his support – "paynfull and dilligent service" in "thappraising the tumultes" in York and promising him "good remembrance to yor contentacon". Within 2 years John Dudley, the next Protector, had Somerset beheaded on Tower Green for treason.

FRANCIS II, KING OF FRANCE AND CONSORT OF SCOTLAND

Mary was less than a week old when James V died in 1542 and she became Queen. She was crowned at Stirling Castle on 9 September 1543.

Mary spent most of her childhood in France, marrying the heir to the French throne in 1558 when she was 15.

In the period 1548 to 1561 Scotland was governed by a regent, the Earl of Arran, and then by Mary of Guise. A close associate of Mary of Guise was Cardinal David Beaton of St Andrews. It was on Beaton's instructions that George Wishart, a Protestant reformer, had been burned at the stake. Following on from this, Beaton was stabbed to death at St Andrews Castle in 1546. John Knox prompted Lord James Stewart (an illegitimate son of James V) to form the Lords of the Congregation and in 1557 the First National Covenant was signed.

The following letter was issued by Francois (1544-1560), first husband of Mary, as King of France and King Consort of Scotland, to Monsieur de Noailles, his ambassador in England, stating that he is about to send arms and other munitions to his Kingdom of Scotland and requesting that the Queen of England give shelter to any of his ships which may require refuge in English ports due to the inclement weather.

It was signed by a secretary "Francoys" and issued at Blois, 4 November 1559.

Trans: "...I am now sending to Scotland a quantity of arms... powder...and other munitions which are necessary for my service. And as the seas are very uncertain and bad, it could be that the ships on which the said munitions are transported may be forced to take shelter in an English port, and I desire you that you advise the Queen of said England my good sister that she give orders...that these French ships be well greeted and treated....and I shall always be ready to do suchlike for her..." (This document came from Maggs Bros).

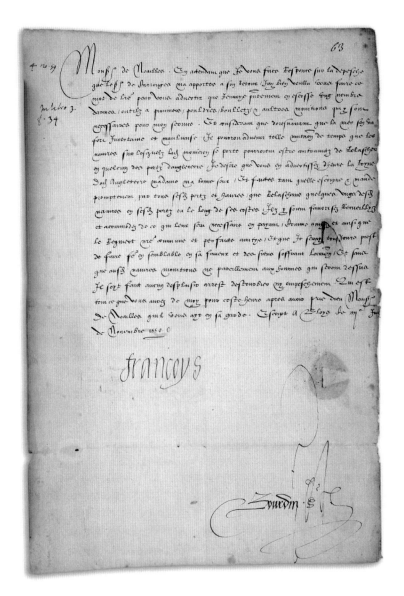

CARDINAL BEATON (1494 – 1546)

ST. ANDREWS CASTLE, FIFE

In 1538 David Beaton became Archbishop of St Andrews as well as a Cardinal of the Church. On the death of James V he became the most important person in both Church and State. The new entrance to the Castle, shown here, was largely the work of Archbishop John Hamilton, the lower part having been contributed by Beaton.

*Letters of **Cardinal Beaton** are extremely rare. Shown opposite is the text of a letter written by the Cardinal prior to the Reformation in 1560. His signature, in latin, is shown below. D(avid) Card(ina)lis S(anc)ti Andree, one page, folio, Edinburgh, 9 November 1542 to Cardinal Farnese. Beaton writes to his correspondent as a result of the incursions by King Henry VIII into Scotland. The letter was written shortly before the Battle of Solway Moss to which reference is made on page 10. A fine letter, not least for its references to King Henry VIII, King James V and Pope Paul III. Alessandro Farnese (1520 – 1589) was an Italian Cardinal and Diplomat*

Signature of D. Card. St. Andree

Rme et Reme Dne, D. mi colᵉ gͤ

Qͣ ma de incursionibus Ab. Anglorū rege, contra sereniss. et Reᵐ
Regem, Dnm meū, eiusq; regnū illatis, ad. s. D. N. in putia
scribo, et eisdemq̃ literis Drationem v. B. omnia ad
plenū intellecturam esse confido, nihil hoc tempore ad illa
scribēdū esse putaui. Fantū illud eam sibi ipsuadere
cupio, omnem meam, operam, curam, studium, et diligentiam
ad inseruiendū illius Amplitudini esse paratissima. ad quod
ita esse toties illa experietur, quoties in suis suorūue rebᵍ
vti uoluerit. interim me Drationi vrͤ humill comendo
Edinburgi nono nouemb Anno M D ✝ ✝ X ✝ ii .

Letter from Cardinal David Beaton.

Shown here (left) are the remains of the Castle's Kitchen Tower built in the fourteenth century. On the right is the rear of the Fore Tower through which the original entrance passed. The Cathedral can be seen in the distance.

The east gable of the Cathedral (left) is seen through the west doorway. On the right is the east gable of St. Rule's Church, believed to have been built by Bishop Robertson shortly after 1123.

THE MARTYRS MONUMENT

This monument, erected near the Club House of the Royal and Ancient Club at St. Andrews commemorates some of the reformers burnt at St. Andrews in the 15th and 16th centuries.

GEORGE WISHART (1513 – 1546)

GEORGE WISHART, 1513-1546.

A POWERFUL PROTESTANT PREACHER. HE WAS BETRAYED TO CARDINAL BEATON, BROUGHT HERE. PUT IN THE SEA TOWER. CONDEMNED FOR HERESY AND BURNT AT THE STAKE ON 1 MARCH. THE LETTERING G W ON THE ROADWAY MARKS WHERE HE DIED. HIS FRIENDS CONSPIRED AGAINST THE CARDINAL, AND ON 26 MAY GAINED ENTRY TO THE CASTLE, KILLED HIM AND HUNG HIS BODY FROM THE BATTLEMENTS. THEN TOGETHER IN THE CASTLE THEY CREATED THE FIRST CONGREGATION OF THE PROTESTANT CHURCH IN SCOTLAND.

The plaque shown above erected outside St. Andrews Castle confirms 'GW' on the roadway nearby as marking the spot where George Wishart died. After Cardinal Beaton was killed the First Congregation of the Protestant Church in Scotland was created in the Castle.

Arbroath Abbey Rent Book

Arbroath Abbey is best known for the signing of the Declaration of Arbroath on 6 April 1320. Amongst those signing this document was the Earl of Ross. Sent on behalf of the nobles of Scotland to Pope John XXII, the purpose was to have the excommunication of Robert I (Robert Bruce) for the murder of John Comyn lifted and to assert Scotland's right to be independent. Ross clan members had fought for Robert Bruce at Bannockburn in 1314.

It was William I, 'the Lion', who founded the monastery in 1178 in memory of his boyhood friend St. Thomas Becket, murdered in Canterbury Cathedral eight years earlier. William I was buried in the abbey in 1214.

Extracts from an early rental book for the abbey are shown. The book bears the ownership inscription of Arthur Grainger, Chamberlain of Arbroath.

Cardinal David Beaton (page 16) his uncle James Beaton and nephew James Beaton (page 47) all became commendators of the Abbey. Above left is the Abbot's House. On the right is the south transept with it's large circular window, known as the Round O, with the sacristy at the rear. The O is used as a navigational landmark, repaired in 1809 by the engineer Robert Stevenson when he built the Bell rock lighthouse, off Arbroath. The sacristy was built in the 1440's by abbot Walter Paniter.

John, Lord Hamilton, Commandator of Arbroath Abbey

The last commandator of Arbroath Abbey before the Reformation of 1560 was John, Lord Hamilton, a son of Regent Arran and later First Marquis of Hamilton. The following document is a grant, signed by him "Jhone Commendator of Arbrothe" with a large part of the monastery's seal attached. The seal shows the Madonna and child on the obverse and the four knights and murder of Thomas Beckett on the reverse.

John Hamilton's later descendants owned the abbey estate outright. An uncle, John Hamilton, an illegitimate brother of the Regent Arran, and Archbishop of St Andrews, was hanged in 1571 for his involvement in the murder of Lord Darnley.

Many early documents were neither dated nor signed, but sealed. This document is both signed and sealed.

Following the reformation, episcopacy was abolished in the Church of Scotland in 1592, and again in 1638, but was revived again on both occasions before being abolished, finally, in the reign of King William III in 1689.

St Andrews was the centre of the Scottish Church throughout the Middle Ages. The cathedral was begun in 1160 and grew to become the greatest church in the land. Beside it a priory was built for the Augustinian Canons serving the Cathedral. Bishops and Archbishops resided in St Andrews Castle which was fortified and built on the headland.

Both the cathedral and the castle, as well as Arbroath Abbey, like many other properties are managed by Historic Scotland. Membership gives free admission to over 300 Historic Scotland sites, half – price admission to other sites, and other benefits.

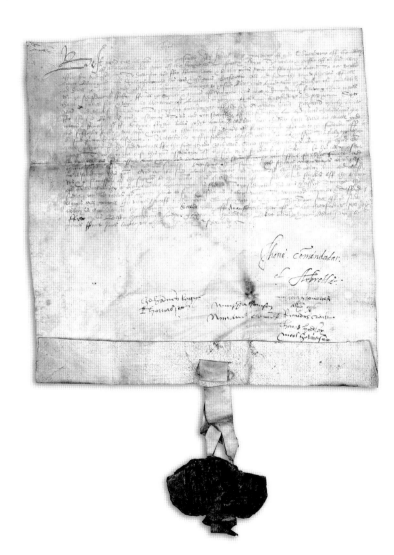

Arbroath Abbey *– the gatehouse range and the guest house. The gatehouse is one of the most impressive entrances, to a monastery, in Scotland. Important visitors to the abbey were accommodated in the guesthouse.*

MARY, QUEEN OF SCOTS

With the loss of Calais by the English in January 1558, the accession of the Protestant Elizabeth I in England ten months later, and of Francois II in France in July 1559, diplomatic relations between the two countries became ever more delicate.

When John Knox returned from exile in May 1559, Mary of Guise was faced with a dangerous challenge from the Congregation, made up of rebel Protestant nobility and clergy.

In this maelstrom of religious and national power struggles, there is no doubt that the most effective player was Elizabeth. Subtle, manipulative and adroit in her dissimulations, she could succeed in achieving her aims while avoiding open confrontation, a path which was, at this time, difficult as England's financial position was precarious. The munitions Francois was sending to Scotland were intended for his mother-in-law's struggle against the Protestant rebels - rebels whom Elizabeth was only too happy to encourage. France and England were nominally at peace, and therefore Francois's apparently friendly tone was fully justified. However, at the end of December, Sir William Winter sailed into the Firth of Forth, where he remained for some months, preventing French aid from reaching Mary of Guise. When challenged, he insisted that he acted on his own initiative and not on Elizabeth's orders. The French, in the meantime, fared badly in the Channel, losing four of their ships with the rest driven back to port.

The following document was signed by Mary, seventeen years of age, during the brief two year period (1558-1560) when she was consort to the Dauphin.

The document is signed "Marie", being a warrant addressed to the controller of her treasury, appointing Philibert du Croc as her first cup-bearer to replace the previous one who had died, detailing the rewards and privileges attendant on the post, on vellum with royal papered seal, Blois, 12 November 1559. In case anyone doesn't know a cupbearer is the person who serves wine in a royal household. It is interesting to note that this document was issued only eight days after Francois's letter, both from Blois. Mary's signature is situated above the seal.

MARY OF GUISE

Mary of Guise was deposed by the Lords of the Congregation in June 1559 and died in 1560. The triumvirate of James Stewart, William Maitland and John Knox ruled Scotland. After the death of Mary of Guise the Treaty of Edinburgh was signed by which most of the French troops withdrew from Scotland.

This letter was signed by MARY OF GUISE. It is addressed to the Earl Marischal, Edinburgh Castle, 15 May 1560, written just before Mary's death, informing her correspondent that the bearer will inform him fully of her situation.

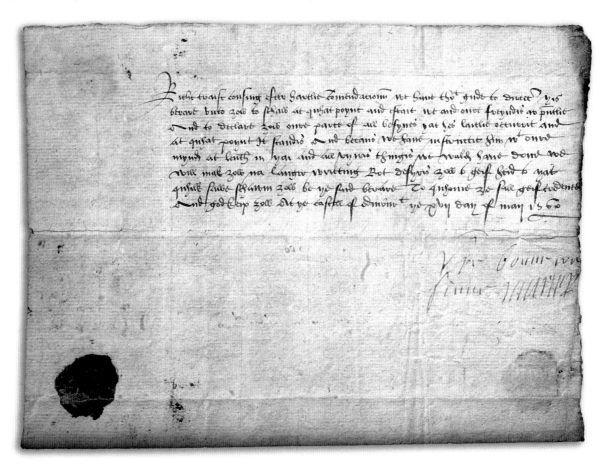

Mary I of England ('*Bloody Mary*' Tudor)

It was due to the accession of Mary I (Mary Tudor or "Bloody Mary") in England in 1553 that John Knox had had to flee to the continent. There he became acquainted with John Calvin. Returning to Scotland Knox was by 1560 minister in St Giles Cathedral in Edinburgh. The Scottish Parliament passed an act abolishing the authority of the Pope with Knox's preaching a major factor in the revolution. The General Assembly of the Church of Scotland was formed.

Mary Tudor, daughter of Henry VIII, was Queen of England from 1553 to 1558. In 1554 she married Philip of Spain. Mary Tudor is the Queen of England who tends to be overlooked, perhaps due to her father having had so many wives and her step-sister Elizabeth I being on the throne for so long.

I have two documents signed by Mary Tudor, that is Mary I of England, who was Mary, Queen of Scots, second cousin.

One is signed by Mary as Queen on 24 April 1554. It provides for annual fairs on 1 February and 10 September each year in Lyme Regis, Dorset. The document is shown here on the right.

Mary's mother was Catherine of Aragon, Henry VIII's first wife. After a revolt by Sir Thomas Wyatt, Mary imprisoned her half sister, the future Queen Elizabeth I, in the Tower of London, later placing her under house arrest. In 1556, she made her good friend, Cardinal Pole, Archbishop of Canterbury.

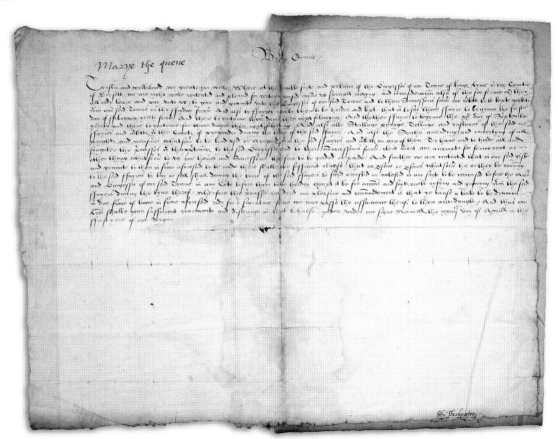

Mary I of England and Philip II of Spain

During her reign as Queen, nearly three hundred individuals were burned alive at the stake, including Cranmer, Latimer and Ridley. Those burnt included sixty women and forty children. Mary regarded those who would not accept her religion as heretics. Sadly for Mary, Philip left England in 1556 and returned only once for a short stay. In 1558 Mary died at St James's Palace and there was much rejoicing. Fortunately she had caught a fever. The result of "Bloody Mary's" reign was an intense hatred of religious extremism and this hatred lasted for generations.

Below is a part document signed by both Mary and Philip, Mary as "Marye the quene" and Philip as "Philipp" King of England. The document is rare as signed by both during the short period in which they reigned together. (1554 - 1557).

After the death of Francois, Mary, Queen of Scots, returned to Scotland in 1561 and there ensued a continuous battle between her and Knox as she continued to practise her own faith.

Knox's reputation is dominated by his opposition to and condemnation of the Catholic Church. However he was positive in his approach to democracy and freedom of thought. His influence on the system of church government is still in existence today; his Book of Discipline was well ahead of it's time and an important element in the Reformation; and his desire was to educate the ordinary man thus enabling him to take part in church affairs rather than have bishops or aristocrats control the Church.

MARY, QUEEN OF SCOTS RETURNS FROM FRANCE

After the deaths of her mother, Mary of Guise and her husband, Francis II in 1560, Mary was left at the mercy of her mother in-law, Catherine de' Medici. After marriage proposals put to her had been obstructed Mary's life became so impossible that she returned to Scotland in August 1561.

On her return Mary found that she had to cope with John Knox, a great deal of political manoeuvring and at the same time find a suitable husband.

Until her death in June 1560, Mary of Guise had only managed to retain control of her situation by the use of French troops. At a time when the power of the Protestant Lords of the Congregation was growing in Scotland, the Protestant Huguenots were also rising in France. It was the Lords' invitation to English troops to come to Scotland and French inability to send reinforcements that resulted in the Treaty of Edinburgh being signed. Not only did English and French troops then withdraw but the French recognised Elizabeth's right to rule England.

What was indeed remarkable was that on her return, Mary retained Lord James Stewart, the Earl of Moray, her protestant half brother as her chief advisor and Protestants who had gained power at the time of the Reformation, in her Privy Council. Mary lacked the military support necessary to oppose the nobles but it was part of her ploy to attract English backing for her desire to be accepted as heir to Elizabeth.

For fear that it might encourage plots to replace her Elizabeth was not prepared to nominate Mary as her heir. What she did do was suggest that a suitable husband for Mary would be Robert Dudley, 1st Earl of Leicester or some other English nobleman. This proposal came to nothing.

Mary Tudor, Queen Mary I of England

Catherine de' Medici and the Huguenots

In Scotland, Cardinal Beaton had endeavoured to reverse the Reformation. In England, as already demonstrated, Mary Tudor tried to do the same. In France, Catherine de Medici, wife of Henry II of France was similarly involved. It was to her son, Francis II that Mary, Queen of Scots had been married.

During the reign of her second son, Charles IX Catherine de' Medici got and took her chance to persecute protestants. After she persuaded Charles to issue an order, the wholesale massacre of the Huguenots took place on St. Bartholomew's day, 24 August 1572. The Pope and the Spanish Court celebrated.

Shown opposite is a letter sent by Catherine de' Medici three months prior to the massacre. Signed 'Caterine,' Chambord, to Monsieur De Ferals, the French Ambassador in Rome, the letter recommends the Cardinal of Ferrara as a Papal candidate.

Following the death of Pope Pius V on 1st May, various French, Spanish and Italian factions had tried to influence the election of the new Pope. However it was Gregory XIII who was elected, influence having been exerted by Cardinal Granvella and King Phillip II of Spain.

Apparently when de' Medici sent a follow up letter to Cardinal Ferrara, her son Charles IX added that if the latter was not going to be supported his recommendation was Cardinal Farnese. It was to Cardinal Farnese that Cardinal Beaton wrote in 1542. Our letter on pages 16/17 refers.

Catherine de Medici died in 1589.

When King Henri of Navarre became King as Henri IV he sought to redress the treatment meted out to Huguenots. Henri had saved his own life on St. Bartholomew's Day by denying his early Calvinist beliefs. After his release from prison he led the Huguenot army, defeating the Bourbon claimant to the throne, to become King in 1594, but not before having to surrender his Protestant principles. Success was achieved with the assistance of 5000 British troops sent by Queen Elizabeth.

The Edict of Nantes

What is significant is that in 1598 Henri issued the famous Edict of Nantes whereby Huguenots were given freedom of worship. During his reign financial matters were reformed and the country's infrastructure, trade and administration improved. He was assassinated in 1610.

In 1614 the Edict of Nantes was confirmed by King Louis XIII but then revoked by Louis XIV in 1685.

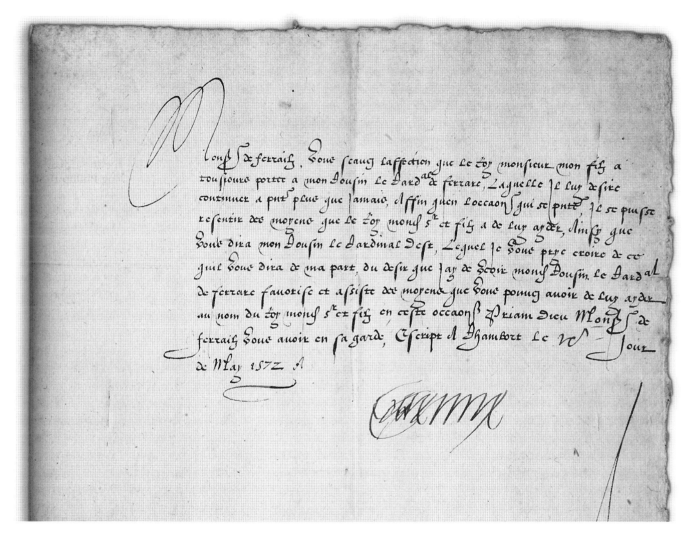

Letter from Catherine de' Medici.

31

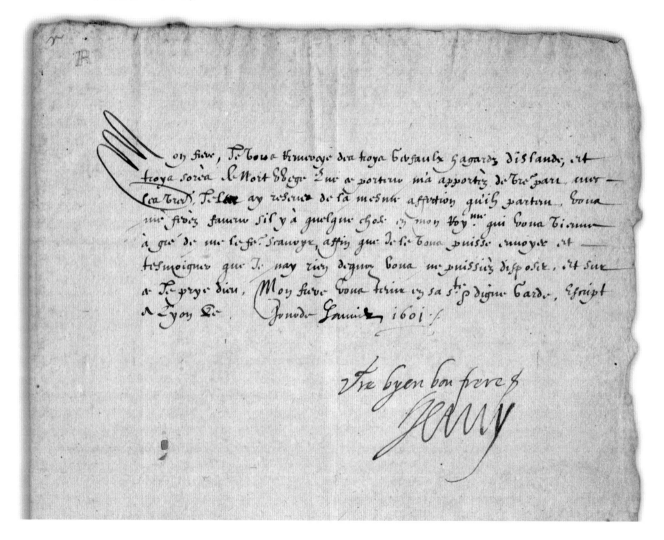

The above brief letter signed "Henry", January 1601 addressed to 'mon Frere' (a duke ?) concerns a gift of various lands.

Between 9th and 12th January 1563, Mary stayed at Castle Campbell, Dollar Glen when she attended the wedding of Margaret, sister of the 5th Earl of Argyll to James Stewart, Lord Doune. Two views of the castle are shown, the Tower house and the remains of the Hall and Chamber Range. The Castle was the lowland stronghold of the Campbell family of Argyll. It was razed by fire by the Royalists in 1645.

The 4th and 5th Earls of Argyll *were very early supporters of the Reformation. By 1556, four years before the Reformation became official in Scotland, John Knox stayed and taught at Castle Campbell. Shown above is what local tradition says is "John Knox's Pulpit" from where he preached: and the John Knox stained glass window in St Giles Cathedral, Edinburgh.*

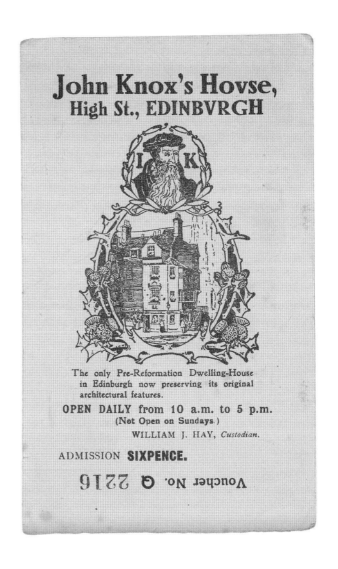

John Knox is believed to have died here in 1572.

The author's admission ticket from the 1950's.

JOHN KNOX AND ST GILES CATHEDRAL

John Knox, born in 1513, so long an adversary of Mary, Queen of Scots, and minister in St Giles Cathedral from 1559 died in 1572.

As reported in the St Giles Cathedral guide, the church was remodelled by William Burn, the architect, in 1829.

Purchased at The Scottish Sale at Bonhams, Edinburgh in 2006, was a snuff box dated 1829 and stated to have been made from the arches of the Cathedral. The inscription is shown below.

"Respect me for what I have been.
The time was when I was a young
and hopeful plant of nature.
In the course of years I became tall
and the birds of the air were
happy under my shadow, and
returned me their sweetest notes
for their protection.
By the hands of man I was cut down
and stript of Nature's robes;
afterwards I became an Arch in the
Cathedral of Saint Giles
and for upwards of Five Hundred Years
have been a cover to the celebrated
JOHN KNOX and others,
Teachers in that Sanctuary.
I also screened alike the Saint and
the Sinner from the stormy blast;
but now I am an outcast from the
HOUSE OF GOD
and become a gazing - stock
in the hands of Man
and part of my remains made a
Snuff Box - 1829"

The sale of snuff boxes could have been an early fundraiser to help finance the alterations!

Like Martin Luther, a monk in Germany, and John Calvin in France, and Switzerland, John Knox, a priest, spearheaded the reformation in Scotland as well as being involved in England. It is interesting to note that all three reformers were alive at much the same time, in common were the years 1513 to 1546.

In 1564, Mary and her royal court stayed for several days at Fortrose in the Black Isle. Shown here are two views of the Cathedral which dominated the town built around it. As early as the 7th century there was a church in neighbouring Rosemarkie. The author's great grandfather is buried there in the Parish Churchyard. Thomas Ross, a shoemaker, lived in Groam cottage, next door to what is now the Groam House Museum. His hand-made shoes, known as "Black Isle Boxies" were so shapeless they fitted both feet. Clearly an economist as well as a shoemaker!

ELIZABETH I OF ENGLAND

In 1565 Mary married her cousin, Henry Stewart, Lord Darnley. Darnley's father, the Fourth Earl of Lennox, was a son of Margaret Tudor and her marriage to the Earl of Angus (her second husband).

Prior to Mary's marriage, Elizabeth I made a serious attempt to stop the marriage. The following document, a passport for Sir Nicholas Throckmorton, addressed to the Commander of the town of Berwick and others, Westminster, 28 April 1565, is signed by the Queen at the head, written in brown ink on paper in a secretarial hand, integral blank leaf endorsed on verso, 'Pasport for Sir Nicholas Throkmorton'. It is also signed at the foot by Sir John Throckmorton (1524-1580). Berwick was a heavily fortified town and the ramparts, built during the reigns of Mary I and Elizabeth, can still be seen today.

The document is addressed to the Commander of Berwick and all mayors, sheriffs, bailiffs, stablers, customers, comptrollers, searchers and other ministers, officers, and subjects, commanding them to give assistance and free passage to Sir Nicholas and his servants. 'Oure will and straight commaundement is that youe and every of youe do not only see him furnished for himself and his servants of hable post horses from place between this and Barwyck at our price but also suffre hym and his sayd servaunts with his money Jewels bagges bagguages and all other his and their Utensiles and necessaryes quietly to pass by you w[i]thout any maner your lett s[ea]rch trouble or contradiction as ye tendre our ples[u]re and will answer for the contrary at your perills."

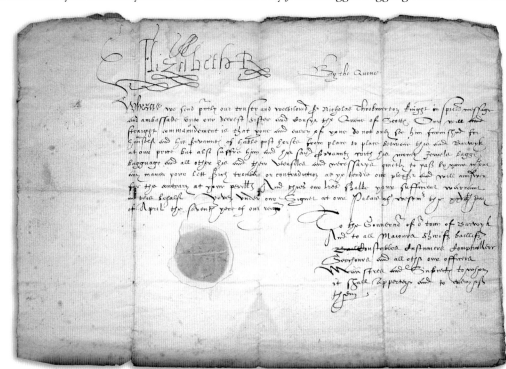

Throckmorton was dispatched in haste to Scotland in April 1565, with orders to endeavour to 'stay' the marriage of Mary, Queen of Scots, with Henry, Lord Darnley. In order that Mary might have unmistakeable evidence that the entire English privy council opposed it, he carried in his pocket the resolution of the council that the marriage would be unsuitable, unprofitable and 'perilous to the amity between the queens and both realms'. On arriving at Stirling he presented orders for Darnley to return to England, and received a promise from the Queen of Scots that the final steps would not be taken for three months. But on 22 July Mary took the irrevocable step of publishing the marriage banns. Darnley was proclaimed King on the 28th and their marriage celebrated on the 29th.

***Traquair House**, Peebles in 1566 with husband Lord Darnley and baby son, the future King James VI. They were guests of Sir John Stuart, the Fourth Laird and captain of Mary's bodyguard. The visit occurred in the relatively short period between Mary's marriage to Darnley in July 1565 and his murder in February 1567. Traquair is one of the oldest inhabited houses in Scotland and was once the home of William the Lion, who held court there in 1209.*

Mary, Queen of Scots and Lord Darnley

This document was signed by MARY as QUEEN and DARNLEY as KING HENRY one month after their marriage. It confirms a grant (given by Mary of Guise during her regency) of the Abbey of Newbothill to Alexander Hume, son of John Hume of Cowdenknowis, with licence to remove tenants. The document is rare in that it is signed by both Mary and Henry during their short period together on the throne.

Darnley was murdered at Kirk O'Field, Edinburgh, on 10 February 1567, following the murder of Mary's Italian secretary, David Riccio, in March 1566, and shortly after the birth of his son James VI and I. One of those present when Riccio was murdered was Jean Stewart, half sister of Mary, Queen of Scots through James V's relationship with a mistress. In 1551 Jean Stewart became the first wife of Archibald Campbell, later 5th Earl of Argyll. Argyll later divorced her.

Riccio's murder and Mary's marriage to Lord Darnley both took place at Holyrood Palace as did her marriage later to the Earl of Bothwell.

Queen Mary's House in Jedburgh. *From here, in 1566, Mary visited the Earl of Bothwell at Hermitage Castle. After a trip of some 40 miles, Mary was ill by the time she rode back to Jedburgh. She was still married to Lord Darnley at the time.*

THE EARL OF BOTHWELL

James Hepburn, 4th Earl of Bothwell, Lord High Admiral of Scotland, emerged as the strongman of Scotland after Darnley's death. Mary was abducted by him and married him in May 1567 according to the rites of the Protestant Church. Although Bothwell was cleared of the murder of Darnley, Bothwell and Mary were hunted down. Mary was captured and Bothwell escaped. This letter was signed by BOTHWELL announcing the appointment of deputies (Craigmillar 19/11/1566) in the office of the Sheriff of Berwick to arrest and deal with rebels. It is dated 6 months before the marriage of Mary and Bothwell. Bothwell died in vile conditions in 1576 following his capture by the Danes.

▶•◀▶•◀▶•◀▶•◀▶•◀▶•◀▶•◀▶•◀▶•◀▶•◀

▶•◀▶•◀▶•◀▶•◀▶•◀▶•◀▶•◀▶•◀▶•◀▶•◀

Craigmillar Castle, about 2 miles south of Edinburgh, is an interesting place to visit. It was the favourite residence of Mary, Queen of Scots, as a minor. Mary resided there in 1561 and she visited the Earl of Bothwell from there in 1566, also living there with him. At Craigmillar Mary's ministers tried to dissuade her from marrying Darnley, later planning his death after her refusal. These ministers signed what is known as "The Craigmillar Bond".

▶•◀▶•◀▶•◀▶•◀▶•◀▶•◀▶•◀▶•◀▶•◀▶•◀

▶•◀▶•◀▶•◀▶•◀▶•◀▶•◀▶•◀▶•◀▶•◀▶•◀

After Mary was captured in 1567 she was transported to Loch Leven and forced to abdicate in favour of son James VI, the sermon at his coronation being preached by John Knox. Although she escaped in 1568, Mary was defeated at the Battle of Langside. Crossing the border into England she was promptly imprisoned by Elizabeth and remained imprisoned for nineteen years.

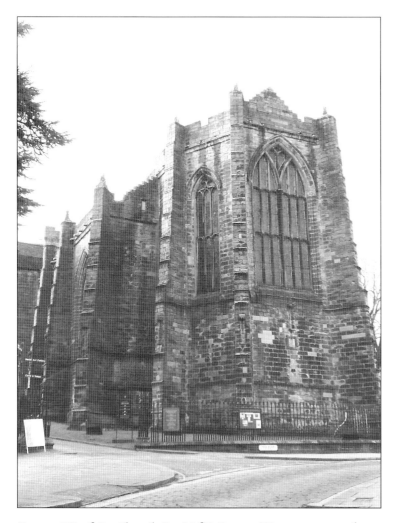

James VI of Scotland. *In 1567, James VI was crowned King of Scotland here in the Parish Church of the Holy Rude, on the fringes of Stirling Castle.*

The Langside Memorial. *A monument erected at Queen's Park, Glasgow to commemorate Regent Moray's defeat of the Queen's troops under the 5th Earl of Argyll, at the Battle of Langside, in 1568.*

James VI and I (The Somerville Plot)

Sir Nicholas Throckmorton (1515-71) was a member of the Throckmorton family of Coughton Court in Warwickshire. Throckmorton Street in London is named after him. Sir Walter Raleigh, who was executed for treason in 1618, was his son-in-law. Two of his nieces were married to ringleaders (William Catesby and Sir Thomas Tresham) of the Gun Powder plot of 1605.

Another niece Mary Throckmorton (William Shakespeare's grandmother) was married to Edward Arderne, executed for his part in the Somerville Plot to murder Queen Elizabeth, the Pope having offered absolution to anyone who succeeded in doing so. John Somerville, who had involved his father-in-law, Arderne, in the plot, was attainted for High Treason in 1583 and sentenced to death. Somerville, in his early 20's, was found dead in the Tower of London.

▶◀·▶◀·▶◀·▶◀·▶◀·▶◀·▶◀·▶◀·▶◀·▶◀·

Thomas Howard, 4th Duke of Norfolk, was one of the most illustrious of all the plotters against Elizabeth. His infamous scheme involved his marriage to Mary, Queen of Scots, and placing her on the throne of England. Both lost their heads.

▶◀·▶◀·▶◀·▶◀·▶◀·▶◀·▶◀·▶◀·▶◀·▶◀·

By the attached Royal Letters Patent of December 1st, 1615, James I disposes of land formerly owned by Somerville and Howard. It is supreme irony that by this document James, the son of Mary, Queen of Scots, is giving away land belonging to the very men who would have made his mother Queen of England.

44

FRANCIS THROCKMORTON AND HIS PLOT

Another plot to place Mary, Queen of Scots, on the English throne was "The Throckmorton Plot". This involved Francis Throckmorton (1554 - 1584), a nephew of Sir Nicholas. Throckmorton confessed to having been an agent between Mary and the London agent of the Duke of Guise. He confessed on the rack and was executed at Tyburn.

It is hardly surprising that with so many plots to replace her Elizabeth's advisors eventually prevailed upon her to put an end to the threat posed by Mary, Queen of Scots.

See Throckmorton's inscription "Francis Throckmorton his book" on a book showing the bookplate of the Prussian Biblotheca Disnievsciana Venus, Aldus February 1516. The book is Ovidius Naso (Publius) Metamorphoseon libri XV Aldine device on title.

On page 44 reference is made to Coughton Court, near Alcester and 8 miles from Stratford upon Avon. The Gunpowder Plot of 1605 was hatched with a view to starting a rebellion to remove James I from the throne and make England Catholic again. Anyone interested in the Gunpowder Plot cannot do better than pay a visit to Coughton Court.

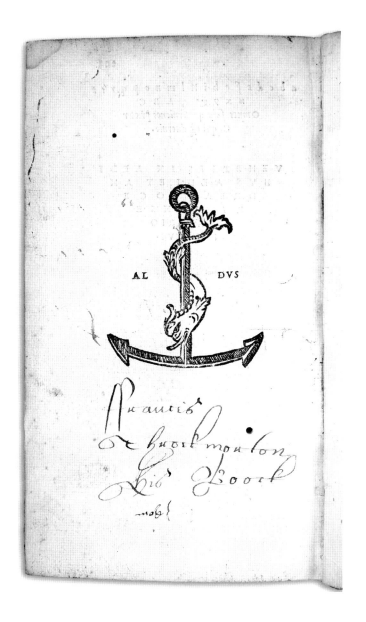

Francis Walsingham

It was James Beaton's praise of Mary which is understood to have inspired Anthony Babington to plot Mary's release from captivity and place her on the throne of England. The subsequent failure of this plot led to Mary's trial and execution.

Francis Walsingham, an ardent Protestant and Elizabeth's spymaster, had become aware of the plot. Using Catholics as double agents Walsingham cleverly managed to involve Mary, Queen of Scots, in the plot. As a direct result of the plot Babington and the ringleaders were executed and Walsingham was able to produce the evidence he required to convince Elizabeth that Mary had to be tried for treason. Elizabeth's wellbeing and the Protestant ascendancy had to be protected. Furthermore should Mary have become Queen, both England and Scotland would have been controlled by Phillip and Spain.

Attached is a letter signed by Walsingham to the Earl of Hertford on 12 August 1585 concerning Lord Beauchamp's escape "My L[ords] of the Councell thought it good referre it to hir ma[jesty]s pleasure what she wold haue don with him, who did order that he shold be [sequestred] into the custody of my L[ord] of Cantorburyis grace", also referring to an examination of Marsh.

The Earl of Hertford (1539-1621) was Edward Seymour, son of Edward Seymour, 1st Duke of Somerset, Earl of Hertford and Lord Protector of Edward VI. Somerset's sister Jane married Henry VIII. In 1552 Somerset was executed on a trumped up charge of treason. The Earl himself married Lady Catherine Grey, sister of Lady Jane Grey, in 1560. Beauchamp was Hertford's elder son, Edward (1561-1612).

Walsingham also became involved with the Earl and his son when the latter entered into a marriage with a spouse of whom his father disapproved Walsingham was someone to whom people turned when in difficulty.

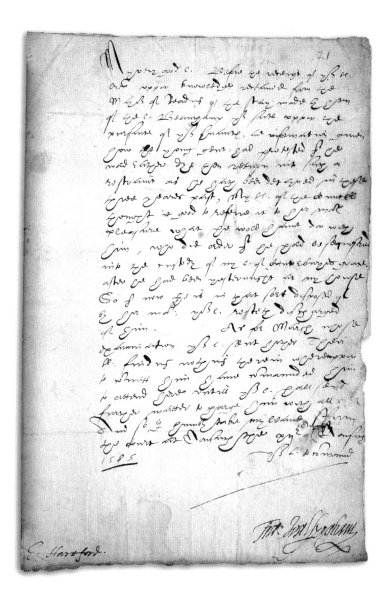

James Beaton, Archbishop of Glasgow.

Another interesting document is this one signed by James Beaton or Bethune, Archbishop of Glasgow. The document is signed "Glasgow" in Beaton's capacity of Mary's Ambassador to the King of France, Paris, 15th March 1571. James Beaton was, of course, the nephew of the infamous David Beaton mentioned earlier, and resigned as commendator of Arbroath Abbey when he became Archbishop of Glasgow in 1551.

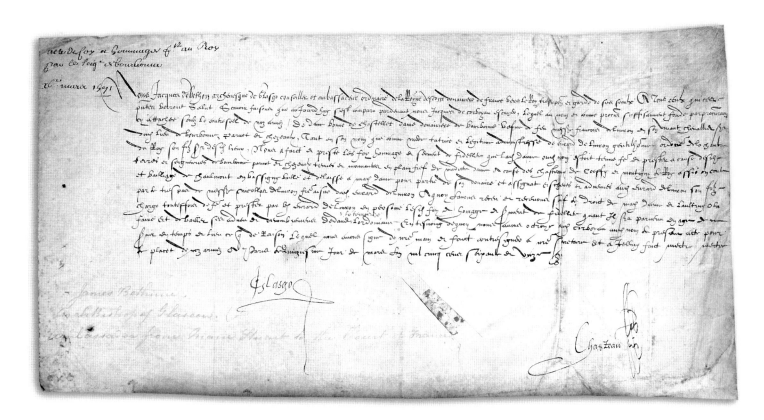

SIR EDMUND ANDERSON

The evidence against Mary was mainly circumstantial, the only documentary evidence being the notorious "Casket Letters". This was a series of letters, love letters stored in a silver casket purporting to have been from Mary, Queen of Scots to The Earl of Bothwell. The letters incriminated Mary in the murder of Darnley and, if not entirely, were for the main part, forgeries. The evidence of the letters was probably instrumental in forcing Mary's abdication in favour of James VI and were used by Elizabeth I for her own ends, by destroying Mary's reputation.

Over the years it was Elizabeth herself who had prevented Mary's trial and execution, but eventually due to pressure from Parliament and her Privy Council, she gave way. As Elizabeth was aware that to kill a Monarch was regarded as an offence against God she looked around for a scapegoat. As her secretary, William Davison, had issued the death warrant he was put on trial.

Sir Edmund Anderson (Lord Chief Justice of Common Pleas) presided over the trial with a view to sentencing him to death. Here is Anderson's signature on another document. Davison escaped the gallows but never returned to high office.

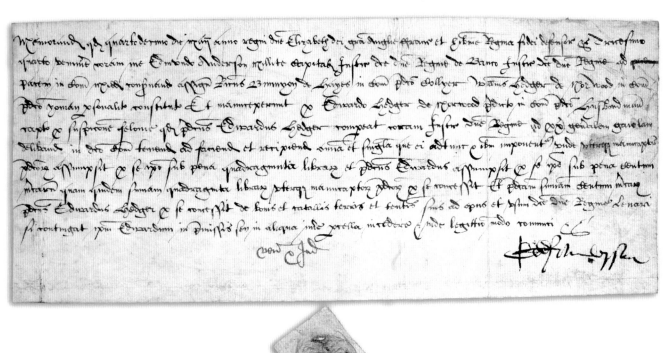

SIR RALPH SAIDLER

Sir Ralph Saidler (1507-1587) was a most important diplomat and one of three English Commissioners sent to York to enquire into the matter of Mary, Queen of Scots, and the infamous "Casket Letters", a precis of which Saidler communicated to Cecil.

Saidler eventually became gaoler to the Queen of Scots at Wingfield; his last employment on matters of state was a mission to James VI of Scotland to reconcile him to the execution of his mother. Those in charge of Mary also included Sir Francis Knollys 1568-9 and Henry Hastings 1569-70.

At the Battle of Pinkie Clough near Musselburgh in 1547 Saidler was made a Knight Banneret on the field for his gallantry in rallying the English cavalry after their repulse by the Scottish spearmen. The Manor of Shelve in Gloucester was one of the rewards he received for his part in the battle. This is a document relating to this property. It licences him to sublet it and was issued by Edward VI, the boy King, in 1549.

The Casket Letters – ingathering the evidence.

When she crossed the border into England in 1568, arriving at Workington, Mary expected to receive support from Elizabeth. Instead, she was taken into "protective" custody at Carlisle and Elizabeth set up an inquiry into Mary's possible involvement in Lord Darnley's murder. While the evidence was being ingathered Mary was moved to Bolton Castle.

At this time Sir Nicholas Throckmorton, Elizabeth's ambassador sent the attached letter, signed 'N Throckmorton' to John Wood, whom Lord Regent Moray had appointed secretary, in preference to the royal secretary Sir William Maitland, the latter continuing to act covertly in Mary's interests.

After referring to a letter from the Lord Regent Moray, Throckmorton conveyed the wishes of Queen Elizabeth that Wood should "repaire hether forthewith so that she might "communycate her pleasure unto you in some thinges, concerninge the principall matter of your being heerr", he also reports that they have heard "of some great dyvorce chaunced amongst the Lordes inn Scotlande, and namelie betwixt the Lord Regent and the Earl Moreton" and other things they marvel at; he adds details of an arrangement for Wood's lodging ("... the towne being so incapable...") and advises him to arrive at 8 or 9 am, Hatfield, 31 July 1568.

This letter was part of the process whereby Elizabeth and her advisors ingathered information – the so-called Casket Letters – the purported love letters and poems from Mary to Bothwell that were to be presented to the inquiry as evidence.

The background to this investigation is that in the previous May, Wood had been sent to the English court to represent the regent's position to Queen Elizabeth. During this time he was sent translations of Mary's letters to present as evidence of the Scottish queen's guilt. Before he would participate in any English trial of Mary, however, Moray had to be certain that his half-sister would not be restored to the Scottish throne if she was found culpable of the murder of Lord Darnley. It appears that the necessary assurance was then communicated to Wood by Cecil, the stance later being confirmed in a letter from Elizabeth herself.

Moray then joined Wood in September to attend the conferences at York and Westminster held to investigate Mary's conduct. In order to protect Moray's reputation Wood pretended to be reluctant to present the indictment to the English Council at Westminster.

Sir Nicholas had already had the thankless task, as Elizabeth's ambassador, of monitoring the activities of Mary, Queen of Scots while she was in France. Following this, he was then posted to Scotland where he failed to dissuade Mary from marrying Lord Darnley. See the Passport issued to Throckmorton (page 38). In 1567 following Mary's imprisonment Throckmorton then returned to Scotland, with a view to securing Mary's release and a concord between her and the rebel lords. Again, he failed.

In 1569, Throckmorton was charged with involvement in the fourth Duke of Norfolk's attempt to marry Queen Mary. After brief imprisonment at Windsor and house arrest he was released in the spring of 1570.

It is thought that when Sir Nicholas died in 1571 he may well have been poisoned on the orders of the Earl of Leicester because in 1560 he had opposed the possible marriage of Leicester to Elizabeth.

TRIAL & RETRIBUTION AND THE TOWER OF LONDON

When Elizabeth ended the inquiry into Mary's involvement in Darnley's murder, conducted at York and Westminster, between October 1568 and January 1569, she maintained there was insufficient evidence to find Mary guilty or innocent. That verdict best suited Elizabeth as Mary remained in custody and Scotland continued to be ruled by a Protestant government. In 1571, the casket letters were published in London in order to discredit Mary.

When Mary was put on trial in 1586 she defended herself. Although implicated in the Babington plot, Mary's household had been infiltrated by spies and her correspondence secretly copied. She wasn't given the right to examine the evidence against her nor allowed to engage counsel. She had no chance of proving her innocence.

When Mary was beheaded at Fotheringhay Castle the executioner failed to carry out the work in an efficient manner, initially striking the back of her head before managing to sever her neck with the second blow.

THE TOWER OF LONDON

Sir Owen Hopton was Lieutenant in the Tower of London between 1575 and 1592 and as such he was in charge of many famous prisoners.

These included John Somerville, cousin of William Shakespeare (see page 44), the 8th Earl of Northumberland who was implicated in the Throckmorton Plot (see page 45), Sir Anthony Babington and the English Catholic Martyr John Paine.

Sir Anthony Babington suffered some of the most horrendous torture ever meted out to a prisoner. John Somerville was also tortured. After his transfer to Newgate, Somerville cheated the executioner by hanging himself in his cell. Northumberland died of gunshot wounds in his cell. By committing suicide he prevented the Crown from confiscating his assets.

A Tower of London document dated 1583 is held being the payroll for the Lieutenant Porter and Yeomen Warders, listing the names and payments to 30 yeomen. The document is signed at the base by Lieutenant Hopton. Here is his signature cropped from the document:-

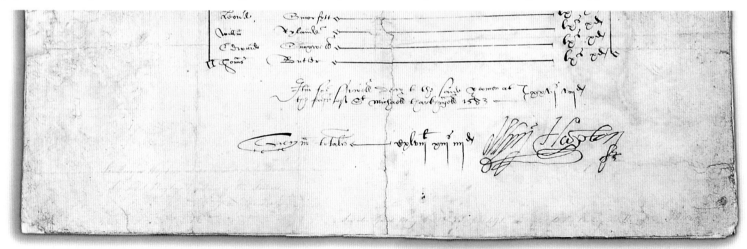

THE TOWER OF LONDON – THE MIDDLE TOWER THE BYWARD TOWER

The magnificent fortress, the Tower of London was started by William the Conqueror and added to by subsequent monarchs. Those incarcerated in the Tower for plotting against Elizabeth or her half sister Mary I must have entered the Tower with trepidation and foreboding. Originally three towers, now two, the Middle and Byward Towers are both fortified gatehouses. Surrounded by a moat, entry to the Tower involved passing through these towers, drawbridges and causeways. To the left of the Byward Tower is the Mint where the coinage was struck starting with the groat of Edward I. Beyond that is the Beauchamp Tower, more about which is on page 63.

St. Thomas's Tower

Traitors' Gate

Shown above is St. Thomas's Tower, constructed between 1275 and 1279 by Edward I. Facing the river Thames with access from the river, this Tower formed part of the Medieval Palace, lodgings fit for a King and used by Edward I. Incorporated is Traitors' Gate, the most notorious entrance to the Tower of London. Prisoners arriving here included Anne Boleyn and St. Thomas More. Situated nearby, to the rear, is the Bloody Tower said to be the scene where the two princes, sons of Edward IV may have been murdered by their uncle, Richard III.

THOMAS SACKVILLE, 1ST EARL OF DORSET

Mary was executed in 1587. After her execution at Fotheringay Castle, Mary was buried in Peterborough Cathedral, but her remains were subsequently transferred by James I to Westminster Abbey. Her tomb is even more elaborate than Elizabeth's, whose tomb is shared with "Bloody Mary", her half sister.

Whilst James VI favoured his mother's imprisonment and protested about her execution, her removal did consolidate his rule in Scotland and improve his chances of realising his ambition of becoming King of England on Elizabeth's demise.

It was Thomas Sackville, 1st Earl of Dorset, English statesman and poet, and son of Sir Richard Sackville, who had the duty of announcing her death sentence to Mary, Queen of Scots. Shown here is a document signed by him as Dorset. This is a warrant ordering the payment of £30 to Sir Henry Lee for the provision of hay for his Majesty's deer in Woodstock Park (July 1606). Sir Henry, master of the ordinance, was educated by his uncle, Sir Thomas Wyatt, served Henry VIII and became a champion of Elizabeth.

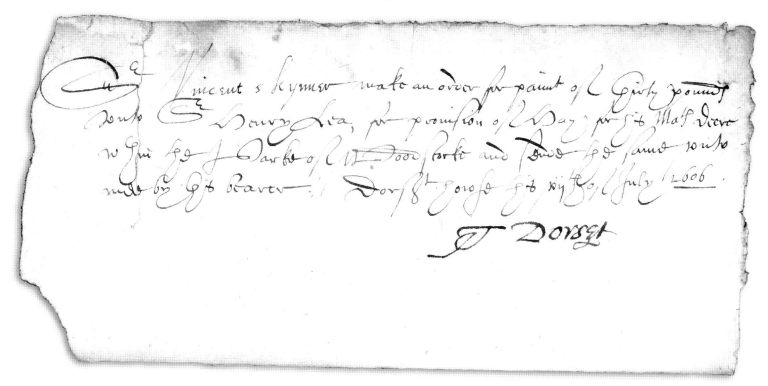

FOTHERINGHAY CASTLE, NORTHANTS

Fotheringhay Castle is situated in the small village of Fotheringhay, a few miles south west of Peterborough, in Northamptonshire.

The Castle was built around 1100 AD and became the headquarters of the powerful Dukes of York, a royal palace and on October 2nd 1452, the birthplace of Richard III. Following his marriage to her in 1509, Henry VIII gave the Castle to Catherine of Aragon who spent large sums of money on it. After Henry divorced Catherine the Castle passed in succession to each of his wives.

The last useful purpose to which the Castle was put was as a prison for Mary, Queen of Scots and it was here she was executed in 1587. The Castle was dismantled in 1628.

Apart from the mound on and around which the Castle was constructed only a section of masonry from the Castle Keep is still on site. It was preserved by the Peterborough Archaeological Society in 1913 and placed in the fenced enclosure shown here.

Following her execution on 8th February 1587, Mary's body was embalmed and kept in a lead coffin until she was transported to Peterborough Cathedral on the following 31 July.

►◄►◄►◄►◄►◄►◄►◄►◄►◄►◄►◄►◄►◄

A final thought on the execution of Mary, Queen of Scots is that whenever Mary left Dundrennan Abbey and Scotland in 1568 arriving at Workington, she presented Elizabeth I with a problem.

Those who didn't accept the legitimacy of Henry VIII's divorce from Catherine of Aragon believed that Mary, Queen of Scots had a better claim to the throne than Elizabeth herself.

At one point, Elizabeth tried to persuade Mary to renounce her claim to the English throne but Mary declined. There was also a suggestion that Mary might return to Scotland as joint monarch with James VI but this also came to nothing.

The above plaques commemorate the execution of Mary, Queen of Scots in 1587 and the birth of Richard III in 1452. Since the author's comments were recorded on page 5 evidence has shown that the bones recovered in Bosworth are Richard's. What has still to be settled at this time is where the bones are to be reburied.

The present **Peterborough Cathedral** is the third Abbey to have been built on the site since 655 AD. It was the burial place of Mary, Queen of Scots until 1612 when son James VI, by then James I had her body transferred to Westminster Abbey. Her former burial place is still marked in the South Presbytery Aisle.

Catherine of Aragon, the daughter of Ferdinand and Isabella of Spain and the first wife of Henry VIII is buried in the Cathedral. When she died at Kimbolton Castle Henry's instructions were to have her buried at the nearest great abbey church and so she came to Peterborough in 1536.

Each year, in January the Cathedral holds a Service of Remembrance attended by the Spanish Ambassador, Spanish visitors and other key personnel.

Peterborough Cathedral   **_Catherine of Aragon_**

HENRY VIII

There were at least two possible marriages (both to Protestants) which would have changed Mary's life and probably the whole course of history.

The first possible marriage was to Edward VI, son of Henry VIII.

On the birth of Mary, Queen of Scots, Henry VIII saw the prospect of his heir, Edward VI, marrying her, thus uniting the crowns of Scotland and England with the latter the dominant force, providing the male party to the union. So Henry sent his ambassador Sir Ralph Sadler (mentioned earlier) to see the new baby Queen and negotiate with her mother, Mary of Guise. The Treaty of Greenwich was signed for the purpose of the union but annulled by the Scottish Parliament a few months later, an event which resulted in "The Rough Wooing" with Henry attempting to get his own way with a series of massacres, burnings, invasions etc., Cardinal David Beaton was vehemently opposed to the proposed union.

This document is signed by Henry VIII. It authorises the appointment of a gunner to the garrison at Hull at a rate of pay of 8 pence per day and an assistant at 4 pence. Perhaps these were minimum wage rates in those days.

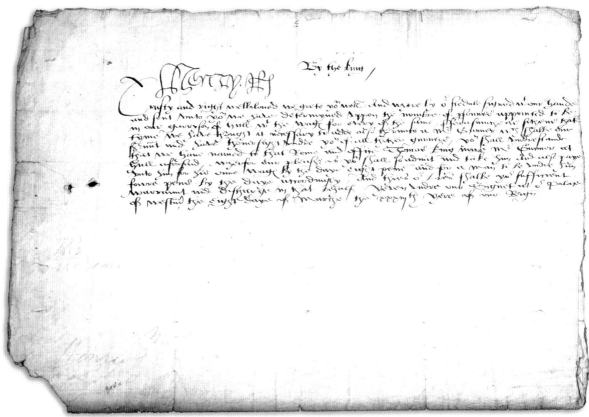

EDWARD VI

Edward VI, son of Henry VIII and Jane Seymour, and one of the lesser known Kings of England, became King at the age of nine on Henry's death in 1547. Edward was intelligent, despite his young years, and continued the religious reforms instituted by his father. His preachers at Court included John Knox. The First Common Prayer Book was introduced.

Edward was persuaded to nominate Lady Jane Grey to be his successor. However, on Edward's death, she reigned for only nine days before being dethroned by Mary I, Edward's half sister. Mary had Jane, her husband, and the Duke of Northumberland, father of the Earl of Leicester, all executed.

Shown here is Edward's signature on a warrant equipping an envoy to a foreign Court with an example of the Privy Seal, understood to be from the same warrant.

Edward was King for just over 6 years until his death at the age of 15. His signature is extremely rare.

In 1547, the English army defeated the Scots at the Battle of Pinkie. This was part of a fresh attempt to arrange a marriage between Edward and Mary, Queen of Scots.

Edward's life was not an easy one. His mother died just a few days after his birth. Anne of Cleves was his first stepmother and she was divorced from his father when he was two. His second stepmother, Catherine Howard, was executed for adultery when he was four.

Because he was a minor, Edward had two protectors – his uncle, Edward Seymour, the Duke of Somerset, followed by John Dudley, the Duke of Northumberland.

The consensus of opinion is that had he not died young from tuberculosis, Edward VI might well have become a strong and successful monarch.

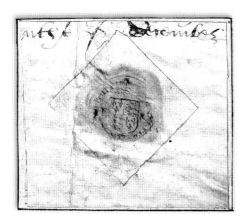

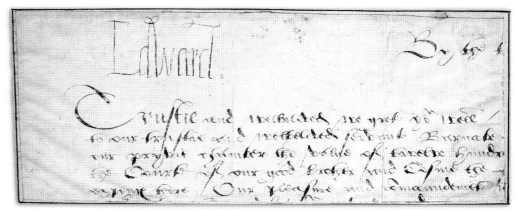

ROBERT DUDLEY, EARL OF LEICESTER

The second possible marriage was to the Earl of Leicester.

Robert Dudley, Earl of Leicester (c.1532 - 1588) was the fifth son of the Duke of Northumberland. Winning Queen Elizabeth's notice about 1558, he received many offices and honours. In 1564 he was proposed as husband to Mary, Queen of Scots, and in the same year was made Earl of Leicester.

The Earl was a longtime favourite of Queen Elizabeth and it was thought that they might marry. Kenilworth Castle was gifted to him by Elizabeth. It is well worth a visit.

Leicester was a member of Elizabeth's Privy Council and one of those aware of the conspiracy to marry the 4th Duke of Norfolk to Mary Queen of Scots. Norfolk was executed for high treason.

When Sir Nicholas Throckmorton died in 1571 it is thought he may have been poisoned on the orders of the Earl of Leicester because of the former's opposition, in 1560, to a possible marriage of Leicester to Queen Elizabeth.

When Leicester died in 1588 he was buried in St Mary's in Warwick. His tomb is extremely elaborate. It is thought that he may have been poisoned by his wife, Lady Leicester, as a first strike before Leicester murdered her and Sir Christopher Blount with whom she was having an affair.

This is a document signed by Leicester in November 1587 bidding farewell to friends in the Hague, Queen Elizabeth having summoned his return to England because of rumours that the Spanish Armada was preparing to invade England. The document, like some of the others, shows traces of wear, but it has to be borne in mind that it is over 400 years old.

Lady Leicester was Lettice Knollys, granddaughter of Mary Boleyn, Anne Boleyn's sister, and as such Queen Elizabeth was her second cousin. Her father was Francis Knollys, Treasurer of the Royal Household.

When Lady Leicester died, many years after Leicester, she was laid to rest beside him in St Marys, which is situated just off the main street in Warwick.

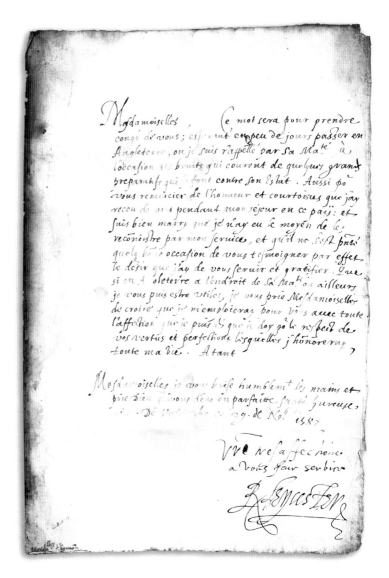

ROBERT DUDLEY, EARL OF LEICESTER

THE BEAUCHAMP TOWER

The Beauchamp Tower in the Tower of London is where Robert and his brother Guildford were incarcerated when Guildford, their father and Lady Jane Grey were awaiting execution on the orders of Mary I. The Scaffold was erected on Tower Green, immediately behind the Beauchamp Tower. There was no compensation for slopping out in those days. There was severance pay given to the executioner by the victim in the hope that the head would be removed in one strike. The term "hacked off" meant a bit more than just "fed up".

The remains of Kenilworth Castle, Warwickshire, a castle gifted to the Earl of Leicester by Elizabeth I and where he entertained her. The castle would have been one of the homes of Mary, Queen of Scots had she married Leicester.

This is the tomb of Robert Dudley, Earl of Leicester and Lettice Knollys, his second wife. It stands on the north side of the Beauchamp chapel in **The Collegiate Church of St. Mary, Warwick.**

James I (VI of Scotland)

The following document is signed by James VI and I.

The document takes the form of a letter superscribed by James as King on 7 October 1612, commencing "Right trusty and well beloved Cozen an Counsellor and other our trusty and well beloved counsellars We greet you well. Humble suite being made unto us in the behalf of Sir Thomas Kirkpatrick of Closeburn".

In this letter the King requests his councillors to suffer no execution to be carried out over the lands of Sir Thomas Kirkpatrick or against his person subject to certain conditions. The background to this is that in 1306, after Robert the Bruce slew John Comyn in the convent church in Dumfries, as he came out he was met by Roger Kirkpatrick of Closeburn who went into the church and finished Comyn off. After Bruce was crowned at Scone the Kirkpatricks maintained good relations with the Scottish monarchs and that was still the case three hundred years later in 1612.

▶◦◀◦▶◦◀◦▶◦◀◦▶◦◀◦▶◦◀◦▶◦◀◦▶◦◀◦▶◦◀◦▶◦◀◦▶◦◀◦

James was openly homosexual and came to be known as "the wisest fool in Christendom". The regents during his minority were, in turn, Moray, Lennox, Mar and Morton. The latter was executed because of his involvement in Darnley's murder.

In 1581, James took control of the government of Scotland. Whilst a protestant, he preferred the Episcopal form so that he could control the Church by using bishops of his choice. However, as the Presbyterian cause was led by Andrew Melville he had to give way. Presbyteries, Synods and the General Assembly were the authoritative bodies.

The Authorised Version or King James Bible was published after 50 scholars appointed by the King completed their research in 1611. This bible is still used all round the world.

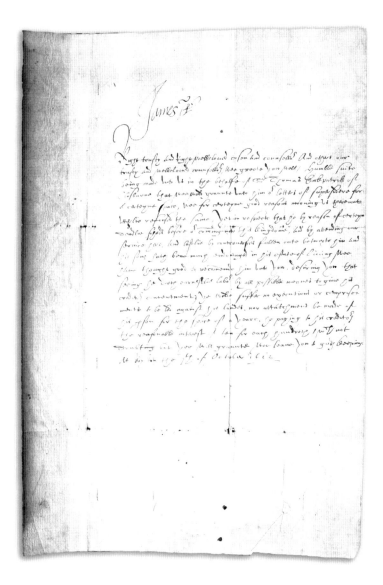

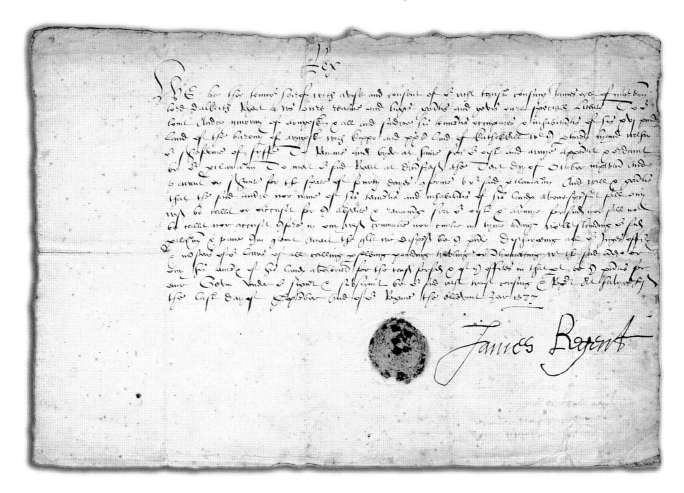

As Regent, the 4th Earl of Morton was the most powerful man in Scotland. The above document issued by James VI and countersigned by Morton grants a licence to Sir Andrew Murray of Balvaird and Arngask (died 1590) to remain "at hame" undisturbed, 30 September 1577. It was Morton who with the 5th Earl of Argyll had drawn up the First Covenant in 1557. Morton was the first customer for "The Maiden" an early form of guillotine which he himself had invented.

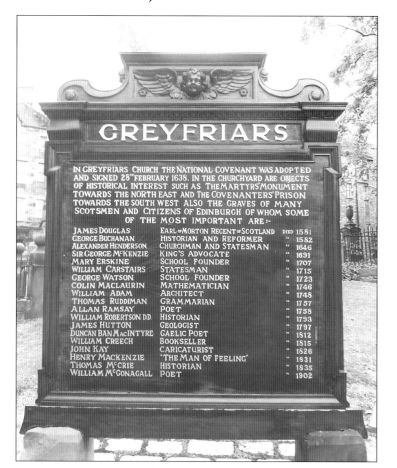

GREYFRIARS

IN GREYFRIARS CHURCH THE NATIONAL COVENANT WAS ADOPTED
AND SIGNED 28TH FEBRUARY 1638. IN THE CHURCHYARD ARE OBJECTS
OF HISTORICAL INTEREST SUCH AS THE MARTYRS' MONUMENT
TOWARDS THE NORTH EAST AND THE COVENANTERS' PRISON
TOWARDS THE SOUTH WEST ALSO THE GRAVES OF MANY
SCOTSMEN AND CITIZENS OF EDINBURGH OF WHOM SOME
OF THE MOST IMPORTANT ARE:-

JAMES DOUGLAS	EARL OF MORTON REGENT OF SCOTLAND	DIED 1581
GEORGE BUCHANAN	HISTORIAN AND REFORMER	" 1582
ALEXANDER HENDERSON	CHURCHMAN AND STATESMAN	" 1646
SIR GEORGE MCKENZIE	KING'S ADVOCATE	" 1691
MARY ERSKINE	SCHOOL FOUNDER	" 1707
WILLIAM CARSTAIRS	STATESMAN	" 1715
GEORGE WATSON	SCHOOL FOUNDER	" 1723
COLIN MACLAURIN	MATHEMATICIAN	" 1746
WILLIAM ADAM	ARCHITECT	" 1748
THOMAS RUDDIMAN	GRAMMARIAN	" 1757
ALLAN RAMSAY	POET	" 1758
WILLIAM ROBERTSON D.D.	HISTORIAN	" 1793
JAMES HUTTON	GEOLOGIST	" 1797
DUNCAN BAN MACINTYRE	GAELIC POET	" 1812
WILLIAM CREECH	BOOKSELLER	" 1815
JOHN KAY	CARICATURIST	" 1826
HENRY MACKENZIE	"THE MAN OF FEELING"	" 1831
THOMAS MCCRIE	HISTORIAN	" 1835
WILLIAM MCGONAGALL	POET	" 1902

It was Mary, Queen of Scots who, after the Reformation, transferred the former Franciscan Friary of Greyfriars to Edinburgh Town Council. The National Covenant was signed in the Church in 1638. Copies of the petition were then circulated for signature throughout Scotland.

The first two prominent individuals to be interred in the churchyard were James, Earl of Morton (1581), the last regent of James VI and George Buchanan (1582), his tutor.

James Douglas, 4th Earl of Morton

George Buchanan

Contrast the stone erected for 'James Regent' with that erected at public expense for George Buchanan, tutor of Mary , Queen of Scots and James VI; moderator of the General Assembly. His History of Scotland, in latin, was the standard account for about 200 years.

***Westminster Abbey**, the last resting place of both Mary, Queen of Scots and Queen Elizabeth I. Elizabeth's tomb is large, her coffin resting above that of her half sister, Mary I. Even more magnificent is the tomb of Mary, Queen of Scots, erected by James I for his mother*

CHARLES I

Being related to James VI and I was a most unfortunate fact of life. His mother was executed and his father murdered. His son Charles I (grandson of Mary, Queen of Scots) was also executed.

Charles was always at loggerheads with Parliament due to his lack of funds. In 1629 he dissolved Parliament and ruled by himself for 11 years, raising funds by raising taxes. The imposition of duty on wine imported and the attempted imposition of a prayer book were two of the reasons for the Civil War which ultimately led to Charles's trial and his execution at Whitehall in 1649.

The final document relates to Charles I and shows Charles in a much softer light. The attached document sees Charles intervening in a dispute between Sir Thomas Holte (1570-1654), a major Warwickshire landowner, and his son Edward. The background is that Sir Thomas was threatening to disinherit his son for wishing to marry Elizabeth King, daughter of the late Bishop of London and sister of the poet and bishop Henry King. By this document Charles tries to prevent the disinheritance and promises favour to Edward. He made him a groom of the bedchamber.

▶◁▶◁▶◁▶◁▶◁▶◁▶◁▶◁▶◁▶◁▶◁▶◁▶◁▶◁▶◁▶◁

▶◁▶◁▶◁▶◁▶◁▶◁▶◁▶◁▶◁▶◁▶◁▶◁▶◁▶◁▶◁▶◁

The Tudor dynasty did not long outlast Mary, Queen of Scots. Elizabeth died in 1603. Within sixteen years of Mary's death, James VI of Scotland, had advanced the House of Stuart by acquiring the crown of England, becoming James I of England, Scotland, and Ireland in 1603 - The Union of the Crowns.

The Queen of Scots is dead!
The Queen of England is dead!
Long live the King!
Long live the UNITED KINGDOM!

▶◁▶◁▶◁▶◁▶◁▶◁▶◁▶◁▶◁▶◁▶◁▶◁▶◁▶◁▶◁▶◁

INVERARAY CASTLE, ARGYLL

In January 1563, Mary Queen of Scots stayed at Castle Campbell, Dollar Glen, the Campbell family stronghold in the lowlands, when she attended the wedding of Margaret, sister of the 5th Earl of Argyll to James Stewart, Lord Doune.

Later that year, Mary stayed with her half-sister, Lady Jean Stewart at Inveraray Castle, Argyll, the Campbell family home in the highlands. Lady Jean Stewart was the First wife of Archibald Campbell, the 5th Earl.

The present castle (shown here), one of Scotland's greatest treasures is now the home of Torquhil and Eleanor, the 13th Duke and Duchess of Argyll. The Duke is chief of Clan Campbell and the Hereditary Master of the Royal Household in Scotland.

COINS (NOT TO SCALE)

Mary & Francis II
Wedding Celebration Medal

James VI
1 Ryal (1569)

Elizabeth I
Silver Threepence (1575)

Bishop Kennedy – Penny
St. Andrews Cathedral
(1440 – 1466)